Edward Elgar

Arranged by Clare Grundman

Pomp and Circumstance

Theme from March No. 1

(Land of Hope and Glory)

Instrumentation

1 – Full Score	3 – 1st B♭ Cornet
1 – Piccolo	3 – 2nd B♭ Cornet
8 – 1st and 2nd Flutes	3 – 3rd B♭ Cornet
2 – 1st and 2nd Oboes	1 – 1st B♭ Trumpet
2 – 1st and 2nd Bassoons	1 – 2nd B♭ Trumpet
1 – E♭ Clarinet	2 – 1st and 2nd Horns in F
4 – 1st B♭ Clarinet	2 – 3rd and 4th Horns in F
4 – 2nd B♭ Clarinet	2 – 1st Trombone
4 – 3rd B♭ Clarinet	2 – 2nd Trombone
1 – E♭ Alto Clarinet	2 – 3rd Trombone
2 – B♭ Bass Clarinet	2 – Baritone B.C.
1 – B♭ Contrabass Clarinet	2 – Baritone T.C.
2 – 1st E♭ Alto Saxophone	4 – Basses
2 – 2nd E♭ Alto Saxophone	4 – Percussion
2 – B♭ Tenor Saxophone	Snare Drum, Bass Drum, Cr. Cym.
2 – E♭ Baritone Saxophone	2 – Bells
	1 – Timpani

Additional Parts U.S. $2.50
Full Score (48006453) U.S. $9.95
Condensed Score (48006454) U.S. $5.75

BOOSEY & HAWKES

AN IMAGEM COMPANY

DISTRIBUTED BY

HAL•LEONARD® CORPORATION

7777 W. BLUEMOUND RD. P.O. BOX 13819 MILWAUKEE, WI 53213

T0083898

Theme from
POMP AND CIRCUMSTANCE

March No. 1
(Land of Hope and Glory)

EDWARD ELGAR
Arranged by Clare Grundman

Q.M.B. 333

Printed in U.S.A.

6

8

Q.M.B. 333

Q.M.B. 333

11

Q.M.B. 333

12